# Festival Foods
## from Around the World

Julie Nickerson

**Festival Foods from Around the World**

Text: Julie Nickerson
Publishers: Tania Mazzeo and Eliza Webb
Series consultant: Amanda Sutera
 Hands on Heads Consulting
Editor: Laken Ballinger
Project editor: Annabel Smith
Designer: Leigh Ashforth
Project designer: Danielle Maccarone
Permissions researcher: Debbie Gallagher
Production controller: Renee Tome

**Acknowledgements**
We would like to thank the following for permission to reproduce copyright material:

Front cover: iStock.com/yulka3ice; pp. 1, 22: iStock.com/SolStock; p. 4: iStock.com/gahsoon; p. 5 (top): Alamy Stock Photo/Indiapicture, (bottom right): Shutterstock.com/Stanislav71; p. 5 (bottom left), p. 19 (bottom): Alamy Stock Photo/Dan Santillo NZ; p. 6 (top): Shutterstock.com/Robert Biedermann, (bottom): Getty Images/NurPhoto; p. 7 (top): Shutterstock.com/Fevziie, (bottom): iStock.com/Edwin Tan; p. 8: Shutterstock.com/Dina Saeed; p. 9 (top): AAP/EPA/KHALED ELFIQI, (bottom): iStock.com/arapix; p. 10 (top): Shutterstock.com/Pyty, (bottom): Alamy Stock Photo/Yuliya Furman; p. 11 (top): Shutterstock.com/AD.ports, (bottom): Shutterstock.com/Kravtzov; p. 12: Getty Images/Noah SEELAM/AFP; p. 13 (top): Getty Images/IndiaPix/IndiaPicture; p. 13 (bottom), back cover (bottom): iStock.com/Rangeecha; p. 14 (top): Shutterstock.com/ii-graphics, (bottom): Getty Images/Graph_1980; p. 15 (top): iStock.com/kohei_hara; p. 15 (bottom), back cover (top right): Alamy Stock Photo/Photononstop; p. 16: iStock.com/yumehana; p. 17 (top): iStock.com/Anastasia Dobrusina; p. 17 (bottom), backcover (top left): Shutterstock.com/WildSnap; p. 18 (top): iStock.com/miniature, (bottom left): iStock.com/Viktar; p. 18 (bottom right), p. 24: Shutterstock.com/ChameleonsEye; p. 19 (top): Shutterstock.com/Mauro Rodrigues, p. 20: iStock.com/BrianScantlebury; p. 21 (top): Getty Images/Chris Jackson, (middle): Shutterstock.com/Elena Yanchyn, (bottom left): iStock.com/davidf; p. 23: iStock.com/SolStock.

Every effort has been made to trace and acknowledge copyright. However, if any infringement has occurred, the publishers tender their apologies and invite the copyright holders to contact them.

NovaStar

# Contents

# Celebrating with Food

People all over the world enjoy coming together to **celebrate** festivals and other special events. Food is often an important part of these celebrations.

Festival food is any food that's shared with families and friends during a special time.

Sharing festival food with the people you care about is a great way to celebrate, like this family in Japan.

Families in India often share colourful food at festivals.

Some festival foods are cooked in the ground in Aotearoa New Zealand.

Special sweets and biscuits are enjoyed during festivals in Egypt.

Do you have a favourite feast that you share with your family? Maybe you'll want to try a new festival food after reading this book!

# Egypt

Egypt

AFRICA

Many people in Egypt celebrate
Eid al-Fitr (say: *eed al-fit-er*).
This is a festival that begins at the end of **Ramadan**.
Ramadan is a time when **Muslim** people around the
world **fast**, or do not eat, between sunrise and sunset
for one month.

Children celebrate Eid al–Fitr with
balloons and dancing in Giza, Egypt.

Having a big feast is an important part of Eid al-Fitr.

During Eid al-Fitr in Egypt, people come together to eat and **pray**. They wear new clothes, and they celebrate for three days! People decorate the streets and houses with colourful lanterns.

Many people share a meal with their families during Eid al-Fitr, including aunts, uncles, cousins and grandparents. It can get crowded around the dining table!

Families share lots of food during Eid al-Fitr.

A popular food served during Eid al-Fitr is *fattah*. This is a meal of rice, fried bread, sauce and meat. People also eat **salted** fish called *fesikh* (say: *fuh-seek*). This is a food that has been made by Egyptian families for hundreds of years.

### Food Fact

**A Dangerous Dish**

If fesikh is not made properly, it can be poisonous and make people sick!

Fattah is great dish to serve to a large family!

Egyptian biscuits called *kahk* (say: *cack*) are also eaten during Eid al-Fitr. They are filled with honey and nuts, and covered in sugar.

An Egyptian woman makes kahk biscuits with beautiful patterns.

The Eid al-Fitr festival is sometimes called "the Sugar Feast" because people eat so many sweets!

Children celebrate Eid al–Fitr by eating kahk biscuits together.

# India

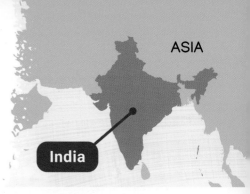

Every year, people in many places around the world celebrate Holi. This is a **Hindu** festival from India that welcomes the start of spring. Holi is also called "the Festival of Colours" because bright colours are used in the food and festival activities. The colours can mean different things – for example, green for nature, red for love and yellow for happiness.

Food for Holi can be made in different colours or served with fun colourful decorations on the table.

Curries are made with lots of different spices and flavours.

During Holi, families share feasts of rice, curry and bread. Golden, crunchy fried vegetables called *pakora* are also popular during Holi. Pakora can be made with potato, spinach, onion or other vegetables.

Pakora can be made with different vegetables mixed together.

Holi is a day of happiness, laughter and fun. It usually starts with people throwing coloured powder and water balloons at each other in the streets!

Children throw brightly coloured powder at each other during Holi.

Afterwards, everyone changes into clean clothes and visits their friends to share presents and sweets.

One special sweet is called *laddu*. There are many types of laddu. They can be made with sugar, coconut, dried fruit or nuts. Laddu are sometimes made in bright colours for Holi.

Two children celebrate Holi by sharing laddu with each other.

### Food Fact

**Fried Sweets**

One of the most famous Holi foods is called *gujiya* (say: *goo–jee–a*). These deep–fried sweets are from North India, but they are popular in many parts of the country.

# Japan

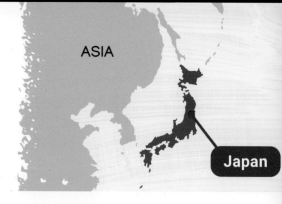

In Japan, the New Year celebration is called *Shōgatsu*. It takes place during the first three days of January. For many people, the feasts enjoyed during Shōgatsu are the most important meals of the year. These meals bring good luck and happiness for the year ahead.

Lots of fireworks are displayed in Tokyo, Japan, to celebrate Shōgatsu.

In late December, families clean their houses together to get them ready for the new year. Then, on New Year's Eve, which is the day before the new year starts, they share a meal of noodles in hot soup. This meal is called *toshikoshi soba*. Some Japanese people believe eating the long noodles will give them a long life.

A Japanese family uses chopsticks to eat long noodles in toshikoshi soba.

Toshikoshi soba can be served with different toppings that are added to the soup.

On New Year's Day, families often share special food called *osechi ryōri* (say: *o-seh-chi ri-yor-ee*). This is a meal made up of many small seafood and vegetable dishes. The food is served in boxes called *jūbako*.

Many different types of osechi ryōri are served in jūbako boxes.

A popular New Year's treat is a rice cake called *mochi*. Mochi are sticky and delicious! They are usually served in soup or with sweet red beans. Decorations made with mochi are often displayed inside Japanese homes for good luck.

Mochi are made in many different colours.

### Food Fact

**Making Mochi**

In some towns in Japan, making mochi is a big event every year. Mochi are made by pounding steamed rice with a large mallet, or wooden hammer. It is hard work!

Two men make mochi by pounding the rice mixture with a large mallet.

# Aotearoa New Zealand

Aotearoa New Zealand

The First Peoples of Aotearoa (say: *ah-oh-teh-ah-roh-ah*) New Zealand are called **Māori**. The beginning of the Māori New Year is called *Matariki*. It starts between May and July, when a group of seven stars, which are also called Matariki, can be seen in the early morning sky. Matariki is a time to be with *whānau* (say: *fa-now*), or family, and people celebrate by sharing *kai* (say: *ky*), or food.

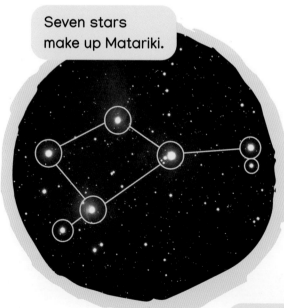

Seven stars make up Matariki.

Māori people celebrate by sharing kai together.

For some families, it's important that their Matariki feasts include vegetables grown in their own garden, such as *kumara* (sweet potato) or pumpkin. These vegetables are usually served with fish, lamb or chicken.

### Food Fact

**Colourful Kumara**

Kumara grows best in the northern parts of Aotearoa New Zealand. It comes in several colours – red, gold, orange and even purple!

Vegetables like potatoes, pumpkin, carrot and kumara can all be cooked outside for Matariki.

Some families cook their feast for Matariki in a *hāngi* (say: *hun-gee*). This is a hole in the ground that is filled with rocks that have been heated in a fire. The food is then placed in wire baskets to sit on the hot rocks before being covered. It can take up to four hours for the food to cook!

Food is placed in wire baskets in a hāngi, where it is cooked by hot rocks and steam.

When the meat is ready, the basket is pulled out of the hāngi so the feast can begin.

Children make sparkling stars to decorate the centre of the dining table for the Matariki feast.

As families sit around the table, they tell stories about the past and look forward to the new year ahead.

Star decorations are a great addition to the table when eating a Matariki feast!

Matariki is a special time to share stories with family.

# Festival Fun!

Coming together and sharing food is important for people all over the world. Many festivals and celebrations have special foods that people enjoy cooking and eating. Some also have special activities, clothing and decorations.

Sharing festival food with family is one of the best ways to celebrate.

Many different types of food are shared during these celebrations. Do any of the feasts in this book sound delicious to you? It might be hard to choose just one!

# Glossary

| | |
|---|---|
| **celebrate** (*verb*) | to do something special on an important day |
| **fast** (*verb*) | to stop eating for a time |
| **Hindu** (*noun*) | the main religion in India and Nepal |
| **Māori** (*noun*) | the first peoples to live in Aotearoa New Zealand |
| **Muslim** (*adjective*) | believing in the religion of Islam |
| **pray** (*verb*) | to talk to a god, such as asking for help or giving thanks |
| **Ramadan** (*noun*) | the month when Muslim people do not eat or drink during the day |
| **salted** (*adjective*) | when food is kept in salt so it stays fresh for longer |

# Index